# Immortal Stuff

Whether these prose poems are about something as mundane as meeting a chemist or as unlikely and comic as a plucked chicken circumnavigating one's neighborhood, one consistent is the wonderful first-person narrator who guides us through the imaginary landscape of *Immortal Stuff*. Sometimes reflective, other times, philosophical or perplexed or tongue-in-cheek about the existential vagaries of what we call life, this narrator always achieves a certain wisdom that only a seasoned poet like Cathryn Hankla can bear witness to. We can always expect the unexpected and original from Hankla, and, in this respect, *Immortal Stuff* never lets us down.

—Peter Johnson, winner of the Laughlin Award;
author of *Old Man Howling at the Moon* and *Shot*

Cathryn Hankla's *Immortal Stuff* offers us a collection of moments, stories, and encounters that form a labyrinth we could otherwise call the human condition. She speaks to us as an old friend we must listen to. If you haven't read Hankla before you'll be surprised at her range—Gershwin, Mozart, tree frogs, Gettysburg—and her music, evident here in prose poems that sing as few can. If you have read her previously, as I have for years, you'll be heartened by the wisdom, clarity, and honesty of *Immortal Stuff*.

—Pablo Medina, author of
*The Foreigner's Song: New and Selected Poems*

These prose poems evoke several of the other worlds that are in this one. Based in this one, they move with assurance even when the topic may be lack of assurance, drifting from the recognizable, concrete surroundings in which comfort is possible, through something like a bead curtain, into realms more privately Cathryn Hankla's, and now, thanks to her multifarious gifts, ours as well. Discomfort is sometimes unwelcomed, but always to good effect. Reading this book has improved my life.

—Henry Taylor, winner of the Pulitzer Prize for Poetry;
author of *This Tilted World is Where I Live:
New & Selected Poems, 1962–2020*

## By Cathryn Hankla

# Immortal Stuff

## PROSE POEMS

*Cathryn Hankla*

MERCER UNIVERSITY PRESS
*Macon, Georgia*

MUP/ P662


© 2023 Cathryn Hankla
Published by Mercer University Press
1501 Mercer University Drive
Macon, Georgia 31207
All rights reserved

27  26  25  24  23      5  4  3  2  1

Books published by Mercer University Press are printed on acid-free paper that
meets the requirements of the American National Standard for Information
Sciences—Permanence of Paper for Printed Library Materials.

Printed and bound in the United States.

This book is set in Adobe Garamond Pro.

Cover/jacket design by Burt&Burt.

ISBN      978-0-88146-874-8
Cataloging-in-Publication Data is available from the Library of Congress

# CONTENTS

MERCER UNIVERSITY PRESS

*Endowed by*

TOM WATSON BROWN
*and*
THE WATSON-BROWN FOUNDATION, INC.

"We're made of star stuff."
—Carl Sagan


"For the perishable must clothe itself with the imperishable, and the mortal with immortality."
—1 Corinthians 15:53


"We are stardust…"
—Joni Mitchell

## ALL THIS GOING ON

Some people clenched their jaws at night, while others kept on bruxing. They indicated winds were coming from the west, cold chills and then hot dry breath. A mixture of aggravation led to increased feelings of buoyancy. But it was more like buoys bobbing than a helium ascent, together with feelings of inferiority and a sandstorm of curiosity. We couldn't see much that wasn't distorted by high or low angles. Even a fisheye ceased to yield perspective. Individuals took walks now and then or volunteered for the army. Crowds seemed inevitable. Feelings of anxiety elicited a prescription for outdoor unity, marches, protests, and a change of the national colors from beige to hot pink, black, and gold. Me, I just wanted a dog like the old one, certain of himself and containing multitudes, everything from spot-skinned spaniel to wiry schnauzer—and, as I've said before, a perfect gentleman.

## BLACK PEPPER

My cat, Tiger, standing tall on hind legs, toppled me when I was two. One of my high-tops got stuck in a cinderblock. At four, I glued a cotton bunny tail on construction paper and called it a placemat. What Mother kept I can't throw away. Back then, I was fascinated by adults who kissed. Black pepper looked like dirt flecks and stung my tongue. I dodged red ash my dad flicked from his Kents. I've already decided to give up *writing* so I can write. To give up protestation, so the giant cat can tip me over. I'm no smarter than I used to be. When I crack my head on the sidewalk, I cry. An honest reaction, but hardly wisdom.

# BLAME ENOUGH TO GO AROUND

I don't know why we ended up beneath the back fender of Mother's station wagon. I kind of remember, but not entirely, flying down our steep street on a sled from my friend's house at the top of the hill to mine at the bottom. Somehow, we veered and hit some ice, maybe gravel. I'm making this up, I think. And skidded toward parked cars, and then before we could blink, we were wedged. My friend was stuffed under there pretty good and took the worst of it. The giant sled belonged to me, or maybe to my sister, so my friend went home crying and I had to bang the dang sled down icy steps into the yard. It felt like my fault, somehow. Maybe the wreck was my fault. I don't remember why it mattered so very much who was to blame. I don't remember being blamed.

# BROKEN CLOUDS

Water, earth, air, fire, a river, waterfall, oasis, ocean, inland sea, a bay where whales migrate to breach and breed. A mountain, an Indian mound, a deep cave filled with wonders by other names, and a range of blue Appalachian hills as far as you can see. The stratosphere, the sky before clouds and after, the O went out of $H^2O$, my breath went with you, into the gaps in deep spacetime where life begins. Like a forest fire burning up deadwood, a brushfire zipping through my withered grasses, touching a torch to every thirsty blade and branch, turning the understory to flame: your sparks reviving the heart.

# CONCERN

Are you concerned about the little stingray creature that flies like a sparrow and has the face of a pug with a black button nose? I am. I am concerned when it snuggles up to me, dropping into my lap, attempting to fold its triangle wings. I am very concerned it's going to start talking.

# CONTESTED CHICKEN

The package passed hand to hand, fresh, day old, and on the third day the chicken sighed before shrugging off the wrapper and beginning to circumnavigate the neighborhood on its own, looking to see who was home. No one is quite sure how the chicken, fully plucked and headless, ably climbed the stairs on legs plumped with saline to my apartment, even managing to raise a raw wing and ring my bell.

# DIVINE MUSHROOM

I'm not sure about the dark orangey shells growing from the maple roots. They could be toxic or immortal (*Ganoderma lucidum*). Like sunshine or joy, reishi cannot exist without its shadow. Like the fungi, I think I might be here to imagine what it must be like to be here forever. My roots are shallow or deep, I'm not sure which, but I am immortal, too. My uses are few and unmeasured by scientific means. My mind wanders more and more and lands on growing things that are true in their own rights, springing up after rains, and have no need of my understanding to complete them, nor have they any use for appraisals of their worth. This is hard on some but becoming less of a burden, just as a shot of cold truth goes down easier on the gullet than the bitter green worm medicine my father used to spoon out to us at the end of every barefoot summer.

# DOGS

We had a layer named Bea. Someone said two dogs were out roaming. Our Bea was kind if not subtle and always first off the straw. Bea's eggs had yolks of pure gold. Someone said they had lost six hens to roaming dogs; someone else said it was coyotes. Long ago, "dogs accompanied only the Goddess, guarding the gates of her after-world...." Our Bea was smart in her speckled black and white feathers, sincere in her pecking through fallen leaves for grubs, comb secure, underside velvety dark. It started to rain the same day our Bea went missing.

# ENCORES

After "Rhapsody in Blue," there's little more to prove. The pianist rises from her bench to fetch some honest thunder, slips briefly into the wings and floats out again, Mozart awaiting. A large projection of her chubby, nimble hands looms over us as she doubles down in ivory. We applaud her again with every sincerity while inching toward the parking lot. But no, how could she cling like a wasp to its sting? We dive to reclaim our musical chairs as she attacks Ravel's "Concerto for the Left Hand," punctuating it with foot pedals, enlarging and enriching the sound. Oh, how her passion rips the air as we fidget! Paul Wittgenstein, elder brother to Ludwig, lost his right arm in World War I and commissioned Ravel (among others) to compose for him, so I know there are other such scores. After her third ending flourish, we rise and pound battle-weary hands, feet all but stomping. What? She doesn't even leave center stage this time but slyly squats again. *Whereof one cannot speak, thereof one must be silent.* "I'm done," mouths my companion, breaking the spell. I quickly trot after him. "They should have warned us," he says, pointing to the program. "She should have stopped while the left hand was ahead."

# EXCEPTION

I'm too short to look into my best friend's window to see if she's there with her sister in their twin beds. I prop a rock beneath their window, balance like it's a wobble board, trying to reach the windowsill and pull myself into position. I cannot. I go in search of another rock to stack on top of the first, but something distracts me, a memory of the dog we painted green, wiping our hands dipped in house paint on her coat. Back then, paint was oil based and not subject to easy scrubbing with soap and a hose. The cocker spaniel stood her ground, then wagged her tail and came up to me. Most of the green had grown out, but there was enough left in her red coat to shame me. We'd all been spanked in a row, and now I was making more trouble. I already knew the kids weren't supposed to come out after dark, that was the rule, but it was the end of summer and I was hoping for an exception.

# FEAR

Fear, my fear, what are you made of? My dear, so much, mucho, it's big as a house, a giant cruise ship like the QEII or QE the first. Large as a continent or the ocean to cross. I step into my hallway upstairs and wait for fear to rush at the back of my head. Truth is, my fear has never panned out very well, and the actual scary situations of life have happened when I was distracted, unaware, not thinking about it at all. The afternoon my father crashed his car, my mother was laying down diamond tricks in a game of bridge. The siren interrupted her play, and she wasn't afraid but should have been. When my car was almost stolen, I was eating a very expensive Christmas dinner. I had no fear of having my car stolen, none at all; the worst I had imagined were dings in the driver's door after parking it in the Hampton Inn lot. Fear, the ritual that keeps us thinking we can control what happens next. What happens next.

# FINAL ANALYSIS

At the end of the day, transitioning, a cold day in hell, the great beyond, when hell freezes over, having said that, circling the drain, passing over, in the long run, considering the alternative, kicked the bucket, in summation, in conclusion, going home, in consideration of the facts, in closing, all in all, meeting one's maker, to conclude the race, overall, treatment impasse, wrapping it up, therefore, the last rodeo, tipping point, ultimately, winding it up, anon, bite the proverbial dust, directly, dropping the body, forthwith, into the light, buying the farm, imminently transcendent, greeting St. Peter, in consideration of one's life and times, hitting the dusty trail, and lastly...

# FINGER

The construction worker could not possibly have cut something off at that precise moment, requiring an ambulance, when she and I were, as it turned out, having our last phone call. I cannot say forever, but at this point it has been thirty years. I should have never gotten involved, it is true. The whole relationship was like receiving an email full of sweet nothings intended for someone else but reading it anyway. I'm happy for her. But for our last phone call to be severed at the knuckle, or maybe it was worse, a portion of his hand, seems too unlikely. I wanted to say, good luck, *bonne chance* with the rest of your life, and I would have, too, if only that clumsy worker had not upstaged my sentiment, or maybe it was the foreman or even the owner of the whole company. I've never heard another word.

# FLUSHING

Water not water, I dreamed I was moving in memory—*hi uncle A.C.,*
*hi Staley*—of course they are both long gone, and in this current no
different from day to day. I knew it. The water kept rushing into the
past, pitching me forward, but I saw what's been missing for some time
now, my father rafting in a straw hat, Huck Finn floating toward rapids.
No Jim in sight. This Huck's alone, bare feet dangling in the river, no
paddle, at the mercy of the flow. Rocks snag the logs lashed together,
twisting the raft's intentions. Limbs snake to stir the water's edge. I
wave, big smile, not yet frantic, but Huck doesn't look up. Water's
quickening now. I pitch a flat rock and it skips, skims, bounces before
it sinks.

# FROGS & TOADS OF VIRGNIA

Little green clinging outside the studio door, wedged in a shallow corner, nearly eye level. Someone called you a toad, but I know better. Your sleepy eyes could have winked at me but didn't. Little green, chubby, stubby, you remind me of the Luna moth I saw out on a limb here a few years ago. Same intensity of singularity, but you are dressed in a lime wetsuit, and the moth, upon closer inspection, was furry, wings so dusted that my touching them meant injury. Little green harbinger, you are not the only crawling or leaping thing I see today, but you are the boldest and the highest. You're probably a treefrog with your own distinct family, because no other frog can be this shade of green in our state unless you hopped a freight from New Mexico, and of that I am dubious. I have the chart before me, and you are nearly indescribable, off the map. Squirrel treefrog (*Hyla squirella*)? I love the name, but it's not yours. You're too large a climber. Green tree-something, my uncertainty of froggy, never toady, it's so natural to talk to you. Pine woods treefrog *(Hyla femoralis)*? No chance of a color match. Barking treefrog (*Hyla gratiosa*)? Possibly. I get out my dinosaur ruler but you wriggle higher, not making it beyond Plesiosaurus. Green treefrog (*Hyla cinerea*)? There is a river below us, but you would be even smaller and closer to the splash. Could you just be a common true frog of family *ranidae*? How disappointed by life would I need to be before saying YES? My choices are limited, and here you still cling, little green, sloe-eyed and determined.

# GAY

Son of a gun, that there is a gay one. Sissy. Light in the loafers. Or butch. Gayer than God, as in, is it possible to be too gay? Too much of a faggot? A relative term. Sort of gay. Look without knowing, and I might not look that way. *Gay* has a longer shelf life than *queer* in the vernacular, and though it pains some to say the word, because they were painted with slurs, to be queer is hipper, reclaimed. Some words can't be rescued from the kudzu of shame, however. Let's let *hillbilly* wander the hollers. I'm looking both ways. Yay.

# GETTYSBURG

Lights dimmed on the diorama in the center of the room as a reenactment movie played. At strategic moments, spotlights illuminated the model battlefield. I didn't know exactly what I would find there, having traveled to Pennsylvania with my husband, whose penchant for violent history felt a little awkward. He had missed all the wars, but his father like mine had served in World War II. Between our fathers, we had both theatres of war covered. Side by side, we were startled by a resounding drumroll, a deep voice intoning, "And suddenly, *they* charged over the ridge!" And as completely errantly we found ourselves cast as Southerners; we played the others in this equation, rushing the hill on a fool's errand. The narrator, of course, was detailing the *high-water mark* of the Confederacy, Pickett's futile push over Cemetery Ridge. Until that instant, I had spent zero moments in contemplation of Southern heritage, and now I was drafted by a phrase into a romance with defeat. Other than having a taste for pimento cheese and iced tea, unsweet, I thought I had escaped indoctrination. Appalachians mainly went north in that war, with their sympathies if not their feet. But even *they* charged over that hill. Ambivalence stirred at the heart of my discomfort, along with a certain disgust at hailing from Virginia, my far southwestern corner conflated with the other end of the state by outsiders. Meaning, the capital of the Confederacy and defense of the indefensible belonged to me. Simultaneously, within the Old Dominion, my region had long been discounted, a target for the war against poverty and energy extraction. The lights came up around us. Blinking, we stepped onto the battlefield.

## GIANT BLACK BEAR

You said the bear was of my making. Over me it loomed, or maybe it rose early in the evening as its own star deepening into its own sky. Stories above where I crouched, the giant bear occupied all of space, as I craned my neck to climb its height with my eyes then tucked my head to hide. I could hear it sniffing the air with a fee-fi-fo-fum. I pulled myself into myself to absorb all my own scent into my pores for fear the winds would betray me. I could smell my own fear, and I knew it would take only a few seconds more for it to waft. I couldn't hold my fear inside forever; soon enough it would attract the bear to me in a roar, each tooth larger than one of my feet, a mouthful of them shining in planet light. Toward me the bear turned, keeping its head high, and stepped over me, and went on stomping into the distance.

# GIANT STEPS

My reaction: intrigue and puzzlement. I trained on piano scales, classical, clarinet in the band, tuned to rock, soul, top forty, folk, and pop. Jazz competed with itself in layers, cascading as it rolled, a runaway 18-wheeler twisting a mountain road with no sand lane. Confounded, but humbled by the facility of the musicians, I did not turn away. The force of the sound made me know that the trouble lay in my mind. I needed to find a more vulnerable stance. Repeating and repeating my listening, I could finally taste and feel jazz swell and bolster, weep and chime and reinvent, a handmade kite whipped by wind as lightning shot down its tail, flowing like a knife, with an anchor that might snag far beneath the boat. Go ahead and pull up the rope.

# HANDS

Hands wave and bless and wash each other. Hands can wash other things, too, like drinking glasses or eyeglasses. Hands are cool or warm, depending. Hands tremble sometimes for no good reason. Hands come in four main colors like directions. Once, a hand thickened like a sauce. It simmered with a whole bottle of table red. Another time a hand grew pale and hirsute. Hands have been said to hold one's destiny or fate. The great spirit's hand might grab and shake the earth. Barring that, hands can fold laundry or snap beans, or make harmonies on a marimba. Hot potatoes injure hands, so can hammers missing nails. When you miss someone, you might wring your hands. You might hold 'em or fold your hand. When you love someone, you might wear a ring, or not, depending. But your hands would run all over them in any case. When you went out walking you would take their hand.

# HEAD TRIP

This is a heart trip not a head trip.

# HeLa

Henrietta Lacks was born Loretta Pleasant across the tracks in my town in 1920. My mother was also born at home in the same town in 1918 and named Joyce. After being dropped in Clover when her mother died, Henrietta had to plant and harvest tobacco until her hands were sticky and stained. Growing up, my mother spent as much time as possible in the public library turning pages of books. In college, she got a summer job there. Joyce and Henrietta both married in 1941, one couple in April, the other in June. Henrietta already had two children and would have three more. Ten years later, Henrietta Lacks died from cervical cancer in Johns Hopkins hospital the year my mother gave birth to her first child. Nothing touched the pain Henrietta endured. Without her knowledge, her cells were harvested and cultured for medical research. The HeLa immortal cell line is still doubling and redoubling in test tubes around the world. Both of the houses where Loretta/Henrietta lived in my town have been torn down. The houses where my mother lived are still standing. My mother died in 2016 of old age without any grandchildren. I asked her to spit into a vial, so I could learn more about my ancestry. She was skeptical but took the test for me. When her results came back they revealed mostly what she'd said, British Isles. I have no idea where I'm going with this. There's really no comparison to make between my mother and Henrietta Lacks.

# HOW TO TREAD WATER

Jump in and walk from the shallow end until your toes can barely touch bottom. Bring your knees up and pedal a bike in the water while finning your arms back and forth. Come on, you can do it. If your head sinks under, stretch your toes toward the black stripe. Bounce up and try again. No, don't lean back floating, using that bubble in your swim cap, or you will be disqualified. The clock will start over. Ride the bike with your feet kicking in succession and let your arms smooth the water. After a while, you can do this and talk to your neighbor and forget about technique, but stay in one spot. Don't swim, or you will be disqualified. The clock will start over. Remember, the first rule is to save yourself. It's like running in place, someone said, standing over us, god of the pool deck.

# I MEDITATE ON MY I

I heard it said in a soothing tone, "I mediate on my I." Or misheard—
*eye*? I've considered doing that, but the I of me makes two, with me
and myself representing three, then there's altogether four of someone
related to me, the I apart from I. Perhaps a fifth and sixth with eyes
involved. It's crowded and confounding, replications or splintering bi-
locations, astral projections? Am I only what I see or what I cannot
see, as in myself? My eyes move deliberately around in my head, pacing
from upper right to lower left, circling one way then the other. Pain
meteors across my brain pan, a gonging migraine, a spasm in the
involuntary actions that keep me alive in spite of myself. I'm some sort
of genius wired to breathe without thinking, a Milky Way horror show
of embodiment as over 5000 exoplanets pile up—gas giant, Neptunian,
super-Earth, and terrestrial—pinging their songs. Spheres glow in
concert in multicolor jabs; synapses fire unconsciously. Take my eyes,
for example: Drifting spider webs or mosquitoes' high pitches resound
in my right eye. I bat gnats of age, dried bits of blood in a cherry smash
of sleep and waking. Whoever truly awakens? Who will take this
middle-of-the-night central-channel breathing and make something of
it worth keeping, measure intakes swooshing past solar plexus, heart,
and throat? Indescribable, wound tight into an opening that dissolves
time and place. Breathe out when you must, to the roots of the old
climbing tree. Come back from death, and witness to us of peace and
warm embraces down bright tunnels of love. Tell us you are no longer
afraid of dying. But what about living? Are you as afraid as we are of
that fullness? My eyes mimic hands of a clock wound forward, ticked
back. Thinking sack behind my retinas slowly shrinks. I rub palms
together and gently mitten my tired eyes.

# IMMORTAL STUFF

The physicist tells his audience we are made of "immortal stuff." He's not brash enough to say we are immortal, but he does say that all our hearts are pumping around iron particles that came from the same dozen stars. Then he says that every day you slough enough of your stuff through respiration, eating, hydration, and losing solids and liquids out the other end that it's like an arm a day goes missing. Every day, you regenerate a new 7%. After a year of this, he says, even your calcium and all but 2% of your fluff exchanges, just as four or five days from now your exhalation in Ohio will be helping a flower bloom in Belgium, and four or five days ago the air you are breathing left Okinawa. In other words, I'm thinking boundaries are illusory and already collapsing as two galaxies draw closer and closer, even if it takes billions of years, finally colliding and enveloping each other. This is why mystics tell us that whatever we exclude in the other we condemn in ourselves. There's nothing better than breathing in, breathing out, knowing giving is receiving, and rediscovering the wisdom of Keats, *beauty is truth, truth beauty*.

# INVECTIVE

It puts everything I rarely feel into perspective to be in the presence of a genuine sack of poop, who's disdainful on top of it, icing his undermining control cake with diffidence. And then there's this: "We do not feel we have been remiss in any way." Well, tell it to the judge. Hey, didn't you know you had to dance a little jig to feed so heavily at the trough? Is this the reason you're wading in this backwater boondocks with no imagination but to step into your daddy's wide Irish soles? So buoyed by delusion are you, understanding nothing of what it means to build from scratch and goodwill. For years you've been known as a bully and a cheat. You earned that much on your own. Our dads' generation went to war, specifically to crawl the beaches of Normandy and maneuver smokescreens in the South Pacific, where their passports got stamped with survival. You went to frat parties and found weed. By the time we first met your first wife was leaving you and your pony tail in her rearview. It used to be dockers and top siders, now it's Birkenstocks and pressed jeans. Whatever. My mother went to high school with your father; she remembered him as a hard worker, a tall loping red-headed kid with manners. You look by contrast like a pipsqueak on a cracker; no matter how I slice this baloney on a cold Monday morning it comes up thick and pale, spoiled, inedible. I wish my mind could wander more, into the wash of a watercolor sky or move along the white edge of a cloud as it disappears. What's really moving? What's really still? What is really real? This moment? The way our paths eventually crossed?

# ITALIAN NIGHT

This is Italian feast night, as it is known in Southwest Virginia coal country. It involves white pasta, semolina, fat spaghetti butter-coated and smothered in tomato-based meat sauce that has been simmered for several hours, even beginning before I arrive home from school so that the brick house heaves a steamy sigh— a luxurious amalgam of tomato, onion, hamburger grease, Italian herb mix, and promise— when I unlock the front door. My father will be working late; he does not like pasta. Italian immigrants have dug quite a bit of coal, but what we have before us is not authentic so much as my mother's version. Still, it tastes good to us.

# JEWELRY

Lost, I think, when I moved out of the loft, or earlier, when I had to pack everything up for the contractor to come back and finish. I'm not sure or I've forgotten, but I did love you. Oh, how you shone, Peridot, diamond cut, set in white gold. The woman was generous with gifts, but I became more and more unable to cope with her jealous demands. I felt as though I were in a velvet box like you, Peridot. I had discarded your original packaging and dumped you into a communal box of earrings where you were lost in the cotton lining, because I didn't love her so much as try to save her, and therefore I convinced myself that one thing could be another. I was left with one earring. I could not figure out how to wear only one, or, without some extreme readjustment of context, how to present myself with a mixed set. In contrast, the woman I later loved lost every bit of jewelry I ever gave her except a ring. Finally, she took that off.

## KAIROS & CHRONOS

As Mom said a couple of months before she died, "I love the wind in my hair!" I was pushing her in her wheelchair.

# LESSON #3

I don't understand this table. I don't understand this coffee cup. I don't understand coffee. I don't understand the refrigerator. I don't understand yogurt. I don't understand frozen blueberries. I don't understand phones. I don't understand comic books. I don't understand the Bible. I don't understand toasters. I don't understand stoves. I don't understand clothes. I don't understand running shoes. I don't understand water bottles. I don't understand sidewalks. I don't understand cars. I don't understand exhaust. I don't understand faded yellow houses. I don't understand bridges. I don't understand west highland terriers. I don't understand people in shorts. I don't understand road signs. I don't understand bicycles. I don't understand policemen on motorbikes. I don't understand sewer systems. I don't understand grass. I don't understand swing sets. I don't understand vagrants. I don't understand children. I don't understand white people. I don't understand Black people. I don't understand little free libraries. I don't understand benches dedicated to dead people. I don't understand trees. I don't understand the dead. I don't understand runners standing still. I don't understand old people walking with canes. I don't understand amputees riding adaptive bicycles. I don't understand humming. I don't understand sweating. I don't understand sunlight. I don't understand air. I don't understand my body as my body. I don't understand my heartbeat. I don't understand how much of me is water. I don't understand who you are. I don't understand who I am.

# LIKE HER OWN

I remember your mother in her stretchy, striped two-piece at the country club pool. She drove like a bat out of hell up Tank Hill in the wood-paneled station wagon. I remember she said, "Beggars can't be choosers," when I asked her, "What's for supper if I stay?" When we painted her cocker spaniel green, I remember your mother lined us up and paddled me like one of her own. My mother said that phrase was hard to explain, and it was probably better I hadn't stayed for supper. Your mother liked to sing, "Mares eat oats and does eat oats and little lambs eat ivy, a kid will eat ivy, too, wouldn't you?" It still conjures windmills and sounds like *wooden shoe*.

## LINN'S CHINESE

Not the white stand-alone building on Main St. at the bottom of the hill, but the grimy one in a strip mall that mostly does take out. That's Linn's. I go in with my friend and sit down. I notice the edges of the linoleum floor curled up and caked with a certain greasy stain like the darkness beneath fingernails after working on a car engine. We both get up as if we've sat in something sticky, glance to the door, walk to the counter. A dark-haired girl comes to the register after a few minutes. "What do you want?" "What do you have?" "Consult the menu." "What menu?" "The menu on the counter in a large stack in front of you." And so forth.

# MARS

I want to see pink banners edged in peach because these are colors that sing for me when I've painted them in proximity. I want to see England reunited with the EU, and especially I want to see the currency of the EU instead of pounds sterling. I want to see someone's grandchild, perhaps my best friend's, become president and reverse every difficulty for everyone who feels disenfranchised or hindered in being here. I want to see a glass of red wine in my immediate future and an episode or two of *Mars*, because the show takes me back to 1969 when I was awed by astronauts stepping on the moon— whether they really did or not— and reading scripture. I want to see you in my room momentarily, and I want to see my sweet Siamese cat again. I want to see my cat's round, dark chocolate face. I want to see my cat's tail brush through my kitchen, held aloft like a test, bent, elegant, tentative, signal flag, articulate, forever brushing out of reach.

# MARSUPIAL

Laying beets in boiling water by their ragged marsupial tails. Watching kangaroos bound from conflagrations that conclude a way of being. Bathing their feet in balm and bandages. Peeling gritty beets and staining my hands. Finding macropod joeys curled in living pouches. Bringing everything to light one thing at a time.

# MORE STORIES

Stories about grandmother Bonnie and her pansy garden with rows of sad purple faces; stories about the weeping man, stolen when he was seven; stories shuffling like cards, retelling the future; stories about rejection and dejection; stories about older male writers who should've known better; stories about faeries twinkling in the corners of my bedroom, magic that came to comfort a child out of the darkness of a father's torment; stories spilled from a fever stick, ever changing shape and impossible to gather; stories that flick the light on and snap it off like a blown match; untold stories like blue spheres that lingered in the trees outside my dorm room—unbidden, palpable somethings watching over us all; stories about the deadliest season on Mount Everest when everyone walked a conga line dodging bodies, stepping over those who had succumbed on their way to summit— climbers breathing, freezing, gasping for oxygen until you tell us their stories.

# MY BEGGAR

I was unlocking the door to the shop as the woman approached. She asked for spare cash. My hands were full. I said no. She walked on, her face contorted, a line drawing to which more shading was needed to make her fully dimensional. After work, I rolled my grocery cart through aisles collecting cans of beans and diced tomatoes, packages of pasta and meat, fruits, vegetables, various cartons. I paid at the checkout with plastic. At home, I unloaded the groceries and separated dry goods into the pantry, cold items into the refrigerator's compartments. Some friends buzzed and asked to meet for dinner. I decided to order the ribs, curly fries, salad with blue cheese dressing, a glass of red wine. My dinner cost almost as much as the groceries, with the exception of six bottles of wine bought in bulk to earn a discount. Our waitress talked too loudly, but I enjoyed my meal. As we were signing our credit card slips, my beggar approached ignoring my friends. She stood at the end of the booth in a holey hat and coat and asked me for anything I had to spare. I opened my hands and said I had nothing but plastic. My friends also said no, although she wasn't focused on them. Why not, I wondered, for any of us could have helped her.

# NAKED CHRONICLES

Poor baby. We could not stop looking at him. We all volunteered to change his diaper, to wrap him in a towel after his bath, and later, we even volunteered to bathe with him when everyone knew he'd pee in the water. Up to this point, I'd only seen other little girls naked, and none of my friends had a brother until this baby was born. A six-year-old neighbor asked to see mine if he pulled his pants down first. He did it too fast, and I never returned the favor. He was in my backyard, so I told him I had to go inside, my mother wanted me.

# NEW TESTAMENT

I have tried alternative paperclips, but metal is best. When you shake it, the magnetic paperclip box rattles and nothing falls out. My students like pink paperclips. My mother left a paperclip on a certain page in her New Testament. If I gave you a research paper, it wouldn't be right without a paperclip.

# ODDER

What's odder than a groundhog but natural to a river? A tail winks—
cotton on, cotton off: Does the rabbit even see it? My rubber shoes
pressure caesuras in grasses that pass stomach to stomach to stomach
to stomach to udder. A stag leaps ahead of its hoisted jib. From the
holt, cubs can venture, mammals after meat. Their HAHS mean halt
and don't make them shriek. *For the teraphim utter nonsense...and wander
like sheep.* What's slicker than a flicker and fetcher to fishes? What has
the muzzle of a hound and the tail of a mink?

# OUTER LIFE

I'm looking at a shadow's edge and finding wavering darkness, a breeze that moves through branches and leaves. I don't have to compare the shadow on the grass to the tree; I feel the breath on my neck. I try to describe it, just describe. The shadow is black and the grass green, but floating in the shimmer, myself in shadow, I discern a dark green shadow. I am a dark green shadow. As I float down river, an isolated blast of sunlight projects an image of moving water on a tree trunk. This sycamore lightshow flickers like a silent film through a projector and has the ratio of an old movie, 4:3. Staying in place to watch this show is difficult; I fin against currents. My innertube makes dark marks on my thighs that I will later need to scrub if I can even twist to find them all.

## PAPER SACK

I've got nothing but a live chicken in a paper sack, its head sticking out. I cinch the wrinkly poke around its scrawny neck and carry it like that. Gravel burns under my feet, stuck between my soles and flipflops. I walk past some folks who see me shining like a ghost. I feed the chicken a few droppers of water during the day. Everything has a right to live, even if its ways aren't ours and its days are numbered.

## PUMA

At the family farm you heard it shriek in the night. Numinous by definition, it slunk the underbrush of unscythed hay fields, the feral perimeters of an unfenced boundary. Limestone caves cored the land beneath our view, and occasionally you'd come upon some scat, check your guidebook, given pause. Your mother sprang things on you from the vault of inappropriate family history. Off-handedly, she thrust upon you a vat of scalding water you had to balance just so. Then there was that time some hunters claimed they laid sights on the black velvet face of a creature (*Puma concolor couguar*) whose tail unburdened them of doubt, yet their shots missed. For me, the high rim of a ravine above a creek was where it stalked, above the road, above my car as headlights illumined a darkness not of the tawny lion, an absence pointing to the thing.

# QUIXOTIC FACTS

I know certain historical facts. I know history is not about facts but interpretations. I know my cat looks like a traditional Siamese with a crooked tail. I know my Subaru is green and it's my third. I know my father died in a teal Ford Probe; the airbag broke his sternum and ribs. I know my mother lived another seventeen years. I know I tried my best to be her advocate. I know I failed sometimes. I wonder about the mysteries of the past, especially about Chaco Culture and the people who built it. I wonder how much longer Ranger G.B. Cornucopia will be there when I go. I wonder if we are all losing our memories a little bit at a time. I wonder how people can be so hateful to each other. I wonder if there will be a grand revelation about the Greys, aliens living in the center of the hollow earth. I wonder if the stars look down on us as we look up. I wonder where I'll be in five years— or even in one.

# RECIPES, LOGISTICS

My grandmother's penmanship lives on in recipes. She measured flour in a chipped teacup and pinched salt. My mother's poignant scratches are preserved on cards or letters. She mainly wrote thank you notes or apologies. My father's florid hand breaks the margins of letters he wrote to my mother and then had to censor, blacking out locations and logistics, because he was the chief communications officer on an aircraft carrier in World War II. I have several 3x5 notecards on which my father typed recipes for chemical compounds. Every now and then a letter goes silent.

## A SAD STATE OF FISH

The pot called the kettle pretty black. Underestimating the present state of affairs, the fish rallied, leaping, even laddering up the stream, leaving the kettle behind charred and the pot unchanged, containing a bamboo steamer. But in the end, it was always for and about the pot. This is unfortunate.

## SAUCER AND CUP

I'm watching him from the kitchen window. Mother stands at the stove in her robe, holding a spatula above the bacon. I sit at the café table in the corner. My French poodle curls up at my feet, positioned for scraps. I'm hoping I can eat my eggs and bacon and go back down the hall to my room before he comes in from the garden. His folded newspaper is waiting. It takes up most of the space on the table.

# SAVING LIVES

I am the lifeguard smelling chlorine every day. I am sort of in love with the other lifeguard. The pool manager is sort of in love with me. The three of us are rarely all here together. I sit in the life guard chair wearing a whistle, sunglasses, and a teeny bikini. It's always blazing hot without shade and miserable. "Afternoon Delight" is our favorite song at the swim club. Some people think sex will save them. I am occasionally distracted when some kid or parent comes to the lifeguard stand looking up to talk to me. They know better. They aren't supposed to break my concentration. Someone could drown. I scan the pool for weak swimmers. The water glares back. "Marco—Polo," kids never do anything but scream. They all sound like they are dying, but really, they are fine. I clear the pool with a piercing blast from my whistle, "Everyone out!" It's my ten-minute break, so I dive into the water to cool off. After a few strategic strokes, I climb out and wrap my towel around me. I choose an ice cream from the case. Somedays it's nutty buddy and some days dream sickle. Whatever I eat comes out of my salary. I am employed after passing lifeguarding and W.S.I. (water safety instructor). An ex-army guy tried to sink me during the final. I passed because I remembered the first rule of life saving: Don't go in the water. I open the pool with a ring of keys and close it responsibly. I hop on my ten-speed to ride home, thinking about the other lifeguard I hardly ever see. This is the most exercise I get, riding back and forth every day after baking in the sun.

## SLIDES

My meeting with the chemist in her laboratory could have gone better. She was what my dad wanted me to be. He was a chemist of the practical kind, a pharmacist. As kids, he and his best friend blew up a tree. He didn't get it, what I was doing, combining syllables into tinctures. The chemist arrived in her white coat and showed me how to focus on some slides of blood, and then we went deeper into cells and molecular movements the naked eye couldn't trace. I was trying to match words to what I was seeing, jotting notes. The chemist was patient, but I wouldn't say kind. "What's that?" I asked her, unable to read the label on the next slide. But while my head had been bowed to the microscope, she had fled, leaving me with a stack of unrelated smears, segments of things once alive, xylem and phloem, splatters as distant as dark matter—or as close.

# SNAKES

Snakes shed their skins instead of dying inside them. People do this, too, shedding their entire epidermis every two-four weeks. Shipwrecked on Malta, Saint Paul was bitten by a viper hidden in a pile of driftwood. A woman found a snake in her kitchen. A copperhead. She had discovered a copperhead when she was a little girl. The more recent snake sneaked through a crack between floorboards, looking for water. Paul shook the snake off his hand into the fire. The woman saw another snake coiled in her closet near her shoes. One time she hurled a small snake by its tail. She learned that babies are far more poisonous than adults. Because Paul lived, the people thought he was a god and tried to worship him. A few years later, the woman saw a glistening mess in the middle of the driveway with just-born squiggles. Copperheads give birth live, not hatched from eggs. Go figure. She bent her head down to read the signs.

# STRATIGRAPHER

Names of buildings change, a fluke of time's ability to overwrite some bricks and sticks and endow and renovate others. Unlike buildings, I defy time. I breathe air continually, involuntarily, in roughly the same spot, only changing job titles, wondering where I'd be had I decided to leave the state at eighteen and graft myself to other mountain chains. Hopi prophecy depends on peoples of various mountains, north, south, east, and west, all over the world, as keepers of part of the story. Have my feet become so planted here that rock strata would rumble the Blue Ridge if I tried to dislodge? My mother, too, was a mountain. "Old as the hills," she said when asked her age. Eventually, it came true.

# SWAN

No one can leave intact, and no one can enter and not be changed.
The heirloom bowl with a swan ever swimming takes a dive to the
floor. He held it close for an instant then dropped it, a sack of DNA
potential potatoes, passed on as a burden, the weight of war and its
fatalistic aftermath, gravity notwithstanding. We were born with
survivor's guilt, backed by the gold standard, fashioned for a life no
one lived. Tea parties were always pretend at the bottom of the pool.
The dinner was cold, the bowl in pieces, just as the grill sailed also,
charcoal ready to sear the steaks. Flames licked from paper bags of
cinders beneath our back porch. Old tires once buried behind the
house sifted under a lush garden but eventually surfaced. He was on a
ship that did not sink amidst those that did, in a kamikaze
conflagration, other sailors bobbing. Inside the house, inside his
haunted head, two eyes, a nose and mouth drawn open in a scream. I
cannot leave and I cannot stay. I am ever swimming around the bowl.

# TITLEIST

Bronze marker bearing the name of a veteran, a father. His beginning, 1919, and his end, 1999. Of jutting granite shoulders and weathered obelisks. Of dates obscured by green lichen and thick spring earth. On his last day, he played 18 holes with his buds, downed a cold one in the clubhouse. I rub my sole against the hard surface smudging details. This cemetery blazing a hill, an edge culture where we measure the impact of human against nature. Where I walk among dead bearing my name. Where what's human recedes, and I say silent goodbyes. Where a golf ball, numbered with a gold 99, wedges against a stone.

## TRYING TO HELP BOB

Bob seemed to know what he was doing when he shoved the burger joint employees inside the freezer. Then he hollered for me to help him crack open the freezer door, to make sure the hostages could breathe, he said. "Hostages?" Sweat was beading down his forehead. "I don't want them to die," he said. "Die? Bob?" I exerted pressure on the handle. It wasn't budging. Bob pulled hard, huffing, nearly crying but his leverage was limited. "Come on," I said, "Let's pull together, you get behind me." "I can't move," Bob said. "My coat's caught." Sure enough, some slick material and goose down was jamming the latch, which explained a lot but not everything. I found a giant cleaver in the kitchen, handy for separating frozen meat patties. Useless for chopping off a coat. Wait, I thought, why doesn't he just take it off? I ran back to the freezer. Bob was hanging by a thread, arms pressing the freezer door, ear flat against stainless steel. The toy gun he'd been waving just minutes before had dropped to the floor. "Bob," I said, "Take off your coat!" It was like he'd been ambushed by aliens. I kept repeating his name, "Bob, Bob," ever louder, trying to get his attention. As if out of a dream, he turned his head toward me, "They seem to know my name, we're fucked." "That was me calling you!" I could have punched him. "It's Patagonia," he said, squeezing his eyes tight. "All I wanted was a hundred dollars," he said. I wanted to wield that cleaver— why hadn't he just asked me for money instead of mixing me up in all this? They had good coffee here, and many times we'd sat shooting the shit. The help never bothered us, even if Bob raised his voice. He could get emphatic, but I didn't mind. I could hear a siren drawing closer. Bob leaned back against the freezer door, back and back, enveloped by his sub-zero parka, vanishing into its puff, the most expensive coat in the winter catalog for sure.

# TYGER

Tigers hunt *in the forests of the night* and like to stay to themselves. Like moving water, my tiger, tiger. My tiger wasn't my tiger but an idea and then a gift and then a furnace and then my heart pounding without a fist and then a loneliness without relief. This poem is about someone or something that really wasn't mine. I wasn't as bright as I thought, in trying to catch its stripes. My tiger was a strong swimmer, preferring the straight-ahead American crawl to the side, back, or breast strokes. In Asian villages, a tiger might be hunted because it's a maneater. I learned this by watching B movies after school. Other things I never knew about tigers: You can try to tame one for yourself, but it won't stay forever even if it likes you pretty much at first and curls up at your feet. Its *fearful symmetry* is its own business. I cried a river over the loss of my tiger. I was reminded of the time I tried to waterski and got right up behind the boat but no one had told me what to do with my arms, so when the boat stopped powering forward, I started sinking down in its wake. My tiger kept swimming away, vanishing into the wildest river.

# UNDERGROUND

An old postcard of the color-coded subway system, "the tube," a sewer of mole corridors, a warren of wormholes, or an ant farm. I had ridden most of the colored lines, a few so familiar to me after a month in the city that I continued to ride them ever afterward in my dreams. The dank stations were often plagued by puddles, ragged edges slicked with oil, dripped from brollies or coat hems. Redolence of peacock and cigarettes. Sometimes, we heaved up from the Underground to darkness above, yearning for fresh air. As I rode up, my eyes roamed across the row of escalators to a descending figure dressed entirely in black. My mind wandered until peripheral vision alerted me to a black umbrella poked and pointing in my direction. His face smirked evilly. Why was he gesturing toward me? What had I done? Who did he think I was? Who did I think I was? Ascending, descending, we crossed.

## VAMPIRES

It's natural for vampires to be immortal, but even if they last for centuries, their coffins transported by barge over oceans and down rivers, they are often caught by light. Coffins get jostled, and sunlight splashes their awful faces waking them right before they shrivel. One seldom needs a stake for the heart or garlic to stuff the mouth. Even if I wake from a dream of dreaming and cannot tell where I am in levels of reality, I am still somewhere. I might be sleeping next to you, the bundle of your leg draped across me heavy and warm. I learned a long time ago that it's really galaxies that are immortal, along with holiness and kisses. Some think of peacocks shedding and regrowing plumage every year. When someone shows you fangs, though, you'd better believe them. If someone loves you truly, that's a real glimpse of it.

# VESPERS

At summer camp, they called it vespers when we gathered around the fire and sang in the gloaming. For a long time, I thought it meant a fire ring, gnats, bats, mosquitoes, and group singing off key. It's really a word for evening and especially for a prayer service that happens after sunset. When I sit in my camp chair at the end of a long day of hiking, sipping from a plastic tumbler, I lean back to see stars and planets spinning over me thinking these are my vespers.

# WALNUTS

Musk of creosote besotted with malt, Laphroaig of the forest; I catch their waft as I clean up my backyard. My garden shoes slide precariously over orb poison, some as burly as green oranges. I stoop to pick one up and see two. I gather two and four part the grass slyly, incandescent as witchy spells. Soon, between twigs and globes, I have two rubber-gloved hands that match the husks in full balance. One nut slips back to the ground, then two green ping-pong balls sift through my fingers, and one so large it could brain someone wobbles loose, then others drop as I try to juggle my haul to the trash container. I pitch them one by one from the foul line, scoring. Bang, bang, bang, they pelt the plastic until they are hitting each other and landing with more of a *thunk*. I try to convince someone, anyone, to make walnut ink. I offer nuts to neighbors, then strangers. If only I had more squirrels, I think. How many squirrels would it take to hide all of these walnuts for winter? Have I enough yard for so many secreted nuts? I fill the city's trash can twice in less than a week. How many weeks of squirrel labor would this equal? It's going to be a long winter, they say, when you want more squirrels.

## WATCHES

Yesterday, today, tomorrow. Watches mark time, a fraught thing. Mechanical or quartz, classic or more precisely: our time isn't moving backward. How could I know when I gave her the watch that it would boomerang? I thought it was a gift; it was a gift. I bought the gold one, the wrong one. She traded it for the one she wanted, wore it a few years, and moved away. When she bought a watch I couldn't give her, the blue-faced watch returned. It pumps like a well until it runs dry. I've replaced the battery over and over. She jumped out of her skin when I made tick-tock noises. There are certain people who want time to stop. If something is ticking, there could be a bomb. I go out in my special suit with my sniffing dog, metal detector in hand, to find the undetonated munitions before they go off. Every so often the dog sticks on a motion, like stalled watch hands, nose and tail, and then I know there's trouble. If I can pinpoint the bomb's location under the surface, I can't tell anyone where it is. I just have to start digging.

# WAVES

Of shiny dolphin skin, a rip in sunlight. In the moonlight of this moment, I can see the day's dalliances as occasional fish that flip themselves skyward. My skin itches from sunburn and a pleasant sense of being my skin completely. Mostly, I have missed those moments. In Mosaic law there's such a thing as a wave offering of peace unto God. I like the sound of it, as waves form and flop unleashing their reverence. Our pontoon boat flaps the surf until we reach the smooth glassy blue, my mind in pools of iridescence or murk, something sharp but shiny. That's where we turn toward each other.

## WHEN IT RAINS

A moebius, like my skin turned inside out and taped together into one surface—I draw a line around the paper which stands in for my skin and it never meets. This is a trick. Here's another: a fortune teller in folded paper. One, two, three, four, you open your cootie catcher to the color red. Red sez, 3. One, two, three. Blue sez 1. One then. No one won. Bored after a fashion. The ticket held the winning combination for the lock. 1003 the combo. You and I were matched, the one and the three. Together we made 4. The zeros were missing yet lent their influence, like a silent letter at the start of a word, an environmental condition, or something like the world bank, there but irrelevant to the moment. When it rains, it rains on everyone, and I am drenched in memories. Merciful Jesus, let's go only forward, never back. That night in the rain we were teenagers in a white panel van. We drove to the town airport. It was small, even cozy. Strobes whistled off the runway. I thought I could hear strange lights sizzling in the rain. We jumped in the light, parts of us vanishing, blinking off and blinking on. Sipping some piddling warm beer, we talked about leaving town.

# WITH STICKS

Autumn's sticks and withered leaves placed into the cauldron with a thatch of bark strips and a bit of faded lichen stuffed around a pinecone. It's called making a fire. At the store, I bought a bundle of split logs, because while you own a chain saw, I don't wield a long-handled axe. I select several white logs from the plastic sack and cinch the strings of my hoody. You take my hand, pointing out the waning brilliance above us as the moon climbs up through the tall oaks. With enough friction or one long match this girl scout arrangement will sizzle, and you can hand me a reason to be.

# THE WORKING BEARS

Everyone forgets about the working bears and imagines only the bears in the forest, bears in their dins, mother bears leading cubs. Shy black bears and brown bears and grizzlies lunge from lonely pine shadows. But I want to think about the first bears I ever saw, the bears riding bicycles, the ones wearing tutus, the bears in bowties and pants announcing the next bear act. These are what I now know to be the working bears, the more talented bears, the special bears who had more problems with depression and drugs. These are actually stolen bears, bears the ones in the forest are looking for when they devour your food stores, mangle your trashcans like tinfoil, and stare into your sliding door.

## XERXES, THE KING

In his time, King Xerxes ruled over 127 provinces from India to the upper Nile. For 180 days he gave a banquet attended by noblemen, military leaders, and princes. "Wine was served in goblets of gold, each one different from the other, and the royal wine was abundant." For seven more days, he threw a party for those who served in the palace. Deep in his cups, the king sent for Queen Vashti so he might show her off, but she refused him. She was busy with a separate fete for the ladies. Enraged, Xerxes sought counsel. Afraid their own wives would also shirk marital duties, advisors told the king to punish Vashti by stripping her crown. The king should find a beautiful virgin. To be so easily replaceable must have pained Vashti, but what is born of vanity and drink dies a hard death. The king issued a new decree: "Every man should be ruler over his own household." When I was married to the king, I always obliged him, until the day a dozen red roses arrived with no note. Our love language called for yellow, so with red I knew the marriage was over. Yet other possibilities haunt me: that the roses were meant for someone else entirely and were either from the king, in which case his love object had changed along with his language, or not from the king, in which case it might have appeared to him that only I had changed.

# YELLOW PAPER

Everything I know about this yellow paper beneath my pen: It's probably toxic to the environment in its manufacture. Paper is unfortunately that way. Paper takes a lot of trees, a lot of chemistry and water, and the run off releases into streams and then oceans. What else? The paper has blue lines and looks like legal pad paper, but it's smaller and bound like a book. The yellow paper holds my scribbles as if I'm writing a book already bound. This is the way I imagined writing when I was a child. I thought writing was like living. Someone sat down and wrote everything into a book, from the beginning to "the end," without any revision or correction. What's done can't be undone. I wonder if anything I've written in this little book will be included in a real book. I wonder if the way I am living constitutes anything like the art of writing, which is much more forgiving. As I sit here, I am writing through my life. My mother read through hers. I've sat here for a long time, probably decades. I've used up a lot of pens, pencils, notebooks, and erasers. I might be a major polluter because of my habit. This paper is slick, which means it's cheap, containing more pulp than rag. The paper overhears and receives my ragged thoughts without comment. I feel good about the fact that it's unable to talk back. Without me, it is mute, silent, unmoved. If anything is going to be done, I will have to do it, and then I can undo it. I can erase. If I write more than I erase, I call it a good day.

## YOU USED TO LIKE PIZZA

On the old house show there's wood putty enough and time. There's a tool made only for pressing the screen into the crevice of the new frame; it looks halfway like a pizza cutter—you used to like pepperoni—and there's a heavy pocketed apron for tools. Several interchangeable drill batteries stand charged, at the ready. If one owns a home, one must own a drill. One must know how to use it. Hardware comes in many small packages, and the wizened man cannot hear what you want, but he finds the wood screw not the metal. You want to drown in fasteners, flashing, and rebar. Washers are usually useless, so you have collected dozens. Leftover paint is never fresh enough to actually use again; stale cans rust in the basement. Maybe it's the masonry brush that makes you want to die today. Yesterday it was the ingenious five-way painter's tool. Tomorrow it will be the shiny HVAC tape you buy by mistake or the odd-numbered third harmonic of a xylophone.

## ZYGOTE

So very small only a mother could love you. There were a few scattered clouds. The sun can't always be shining. The ovum isn't just bluebirds and cotton candy, you know. Shadows are important, I've learned, especially when the sun's highest in the sky.

# ACKNOWLEDGMENTS

My heartfelt thanks to Peter Johnson, Pablo Medina, and Henry Taylor for their comments, and to Bonnie's Poetry Workshop for revision suggestions on several of these poems. My thanks also to the editors of the following publications where certain poems first appeared:

*Artemis*: "Puma"

*On the Seawall*, www.ronslate.com: "Recipes, Logistics," "Saucer and Cup," "Giant Black Bear," "Divine Mushroom," "Encores."

## *Notes*

In "Dogs," the quoted material is from *The Woman's Encyclopedia of Myths and Secrets* by Barbara G. Walker, HarperCollins Publishers, 1983: 240.

In "Encores," the italicized text comes from the conclusion of philosopher Ludwig Wittgenstein's *Tractatus Logico-Philosophicus.*

In "Odder," the italicized text comes from Zechariah 10:2 (RSV).

"Tyger" contains two phrases borrowed from William Blake's "The Tyger."

In "Xerxes, the King," the quotation comes from Esther 1:7, 22 (NIV).

Tom Chi uses the phrase "immortal stuff" during his presentation, "Everything is Connected":
https://www.youtube.com/watch?v=zyr4qORDu2A

# ABOUT THE AUTHOR

Cathryn Hankla is a native of Southwest Virginia and the author of more than fifteen books of poetry, fiction, and nonfiction. *Galaxies, Lost Places: On Losing and Finding Home,* and *Not Xanadu* are also published by Mercer University Press. Hankla is professor emerita of English & Creative Writing, Hollins University, and the poetry editor of *The Hollins Critic.* She writes and paints in Roanoke, Virginia. For more information see www.cathrynhankla.com.